All Aboard America

White House

A Buddy Book
by
Julie Murray

ABDO
Publishing Company

VISIT US AT
www.abdopub.com

Published by Buddy Books, an imprint of ABDO Publishing Company, 4940 Viking Drive, Edina, Minnesota 55435. Copyright © 2003 by Abdo Consulting Group, Inc. International copyrights reserved in all countries. No part of this book may be reproduced in any form without written permission from the publisher.

Printed in the United States.

Edited by: Christy DeVillier
Contributing Editors: Matt Ray, Michael P. Goecke
Graphic Design: Deborah Coldiron
Image Research: Deborah Coldiron
Cover Photograph: Getty Images
Interior Photographs: Historic American Buildings Survey, Library of Congress, Photospin

Library of Congress Cataloging-in-Publication Data

Murray, Julie, 1969-
   White House / Julie Murray.
      p. cm. — (All aboard America)
   Includes bibliographical references and index.
   Summary: An introduction to the home of the United States president, including its history and design and construction.
   ISBN 1-57765-668-7
      1. White House (Washington, D.C.)—Juvenile literature. 2. Washington (D.C.)—Buildings, structures, etc.—Juvenile literature. [1. White House (Washington, D.C.) 2. Washington (D.C.)—Buildings, structures, etc.] I. Title.

F204.W5 M87 2002
975.3—dc21

                                                2001055243

Table of Contents

The President's House

The White House is where the United States president lives. The President's House is in the United States **capital** city. A capital city is where government leaders meet.

Washington, D.C. is the capital of the United States. It is near Maryland and the Potomac River.

Washington, D.C.

The White House is in Washington, D.C.

In 1789, George Washington became the United States's first president. Back then, the United States did not have a home for the president. Washington worked hard to have a President's House built.

Washington, D.C. is named after George Washington.

George Washington first chose Charles Pierre L'Enfant to build the President's House. He was a French **architect**. L'Enfant wanted to build a Presidential Palace. But L'Enfant's palace cost too much money.

George Washington decided to hire a
new **architect**. He held a contest to find
the best plan for the President's House.
Washington received nine plans. He
liked James Hoban's plan the best. So,
James Hoban became the architect of
the President's House.

The White House is made of stones and large bricks.

The building of the President's House began in 1792. In 1793, the building plans changed. A big stone house cost too much money. They decided to use more bricks and fewer stones.

A picture of the White House in 1807.

The White House was finished in 1800. At this time, it was 168 feet (51 m) long and 85 feet (26 m) deep.

George Washington never lived in the White House. He died in 1799. John Adams was the first president to live there. He is America's second president.

President John Adams

Detour

Did You Know?

People did not always call the President's House the "White House." President Theodore Roosevelt gave the White House its name. He was president from 1901 to 1909.

In 1814, Great Britain attacked Washington, D.C. The British set fire to the White House. At this time, James Madison was president. His wife, Dolly Madison, saved many things from burning. A special painting of George Washington was one of them.

Dolly Madison (left) saved many things from the White House fire (right) of 1814.

CHAPTER 5

A Better White House

The White House has changed a lot over the years. In the late 1800s, the White House got telephones and **electricity**. In 1902, President Theodore Roosevelt made the White House bigger. He hired workers to build a new West Wing.

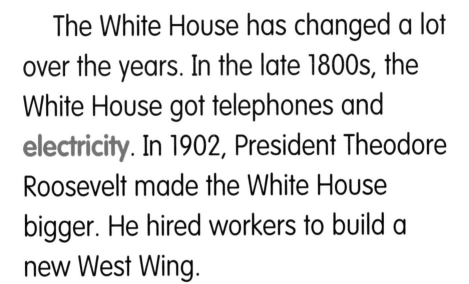
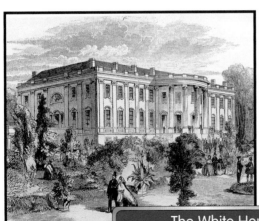

The White House of 1858 (left) was smaller than it is today (right).

President Harry S. Truman

By 1945, the old White House needed a lot of repairs. So, President Truman **restored** much of the White House. Today, the White House has a bowling alley and a movie theater.

The East Room is the biggest room in the White House. Weddings, dances, and **press conferences** take place there. Big dinners take place in the State Dining Room.

The East Room

Detour ⬇

Did You Know?

Union soldiers camped in the East Room of the White House during the Civil War.

The president's family lives on the second floor. Bedrooms, family rooms, and a kitchen are there. The famous Lincoln Bedroom is there, too. Abraham Lincoln signed the **Emancipation Proclamation** in this room. He did not sleep in there.

President Abraham Lincoln

The Oval Office is in the West Wing of the White House. This is the president's office. This famous room is named after its oval shape. The president meets with important world leaders in the Oval Office. Sometimes, the president gives speeches from this room, too.

The Oval Office

A White House Tour

Here are some more famous rooms in the White House.

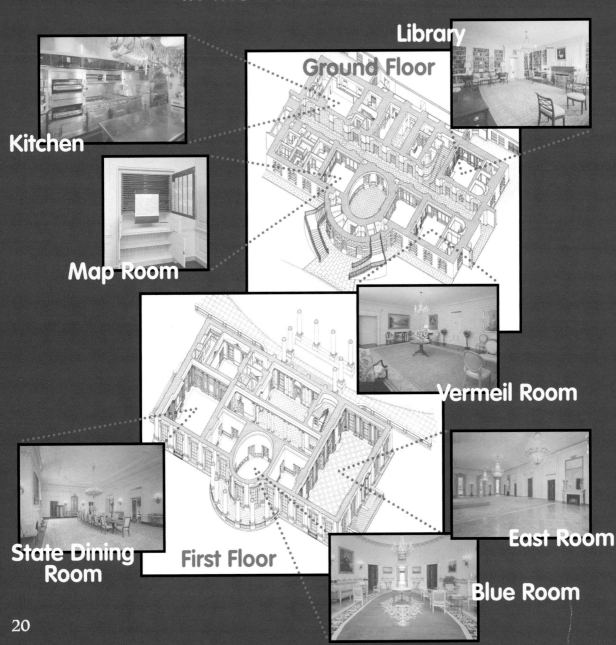

Library

Ground Floor

Kitchen

Map Room

Vermeil Room

State Dining Room

First Floor

East Room

Blue Room

Students often take field trips to the White House.

The White House has been an important part of the United States for more than 200 years. More than one million people visit the White House every year. The White House address is 1600 Pennsylvania Avenue. It is open to visitors and free of charge.

Important Words

architect (AR-kuh-tekt) a person who designs buildings, bridges, and other things.

capital (KAP-it-tull) a city where government leaders meet.

electricity (ee-lek-TRISS-it-tee) what powers electric things like lights and televisions.

Emancipation Proclamation (ee-MAN-si-PAY-shun PROK-luh-MAY-shun) President Lincoln wrote this famous paper that helped to free many slaves.

press conference (press KON-fer-unss) a meeting with reporters from newspapers and radio and television stations.

restore (ree-STOR) to make an old house look like new again.

Web Sites

Would you like to learn more about the White House?

Please visit ABDO Publishing Company on the information superhighway to find web site links about the White House. These links are routinely monitored and updated to provide the most current information available.

www.abdopub.com

Index